NOTEBOOK OF
ANTON CHEKHOV

THE TALES OF CHEKHOV

Volume 1   *The Darling and Other Stories*

Volume 2   *The Duel and Other Stories*

Volume 3   *The Lady with the Dog and Other Stories*

Volume 4   *The Party and Other Stories*

Volume 5   *The Wife and Other Stories*

Volume 6   *The Witch and Other Stories*

Volume 7   *The Bishop and Other Stories*

Volume 8   *The Chorus Girl and Other Stories*

Volume 9   *The Schoolmistress and Other Stories*

Volume 10   *The Horse-Stealers and Other Stories*

Volume 11   *The Schoolmaster and Other Stories*

Volume 12   *The Cook's Wedding and Other Stories*

Volume 13   *Love and Other Stories*

ALSO BY ANTON CHEKHOV

The Unknown Chekhov

Notebook of Anton Chekhov

NOTEBOOK OF ANTON CHEKHOV

Translated by
S. S. KOTELIANSKY
AND LEONARD WOOLF

The Ecco Press
New York

PRINTED IN THE UNITED STATES OF AMERICA

The Ecco Press logo by Ahmed Yacoubi

Library of Congress Cataloging in Publication Data
Chekhov, Anton Pavlovich, 1860-1904.
Note-book of Anton Chekhov.
Reprint. Originally published: New York : B.W. Huebsch, c1921.
1. Chekhov, Anton Pavlovich, 1860-1904—Notebooks, sketchbooks, etc.
I. Koteliansky, S. S. (Samuel Solomonovitch), 1880-1955.
II. Woolf, Leonard, 1880-1969.
III. Title.   IV. Title: Notebook of Anton Chekhov.
PG3456.A16K6   1987   891.78'303   87-6834
ISBN 0-88001-145-9   (pbk.)

*Publication of this book is made possible in part
by a grant from the National Endowment for the Arts*

THIS volume consists of notes, themes, and sketches for works which Anton Chekhov intended to write, and are characteristic of the methods of his artistic production. Among his papers was found a series of sheets in a special cover with the inscription: "Themes, thoughts, notes, and fragments." Madame L. O. Knipper-Chekhov, Chekhov's wife, also possesses his note-book, in which he entered separate themes for his future work, quotations which he liked, etc. If he used any material, he used to strike it out in the note-book. The significance which Chekhov attributed to this material may be judged from the fact that he re-copied most of it into a special copy book.

CONTENTS

PAGE

ANTON CHEKHOV'S DIARY 1

ANTON CHEKHOV'S NOTEBOOKS . . 13

THEMES, THOUGHTS,
   NOTES AND FRAGMENTS 127

ANTON CHEKHOV'S DIARY.
1896

My neighbor V. N. S. told me that his uncle Fet-Shenshin, the famous poet, when driving through the Mokhovaia Street, would invariably let down the window of his carriage and spit at the University. He would expectorate and spit: Bah! His coachman got so used to this that every time he drove past the University, he would stop.

In January I was in Petersburg and stayed with Souvorin. I often saw Potapenko. Met Korolenko. I often went to the Maly Theatre. As Alexander [Chekhov's brother] came downstairs one day, B. V. G. simultaneously came out of the editorial office of the *Novoye Vremya* and said to me indignantly: "Why do you set the old man (i. e. Souvorin) against Burenin?" I have never spoken ill of the contributors to the *Novoye Vremya* in Souvorin's presence, although I have the deepest disrespect for the majority of them.

In February, passing through Moscow, I went to see L. N. Tolstoi. He was irri-

[1]

tated, made stinging remarks about the *dé-cadents*, and for an hour and a half argued with B. Tchitcherin, who, I thought, talked nonsense all the time. Tatyana and Mary [Tolstoi's daughters] laid out a patience; they both wished, and asked me to pick a card out; I picked out the ace of spades separately for each of them, and that annoyed them. By accident there were two aces of spades in the pack. Both of them are extraordinarily sympathetic, and their attitude to their father is touching. The countess denounced the painter Gé all the evening. She too was irritated.

May 5. The sexton Ivan Nicolayevitch brought my portrait, which he has painted from a photograph. In the evening V. N. S. brought his friend N. He is director of the Foreign Department. . . editor of a magazine. . . and doctor of medicine. He gives the impression of being an unusually stupid person and a reptile. He said: "There's nothing more pernicious on earth than a rascally liberal paper," and told us that, apparently, the peasants whom he doctors, having got his advice and medicine free of charge, ask him for a tip. He and S.

speak of the peasants with exasperation and loathing.

June 1. I was at the Vagankov Cemetery and saw the graves there of the victims of the Khodinka. [During the coronation of Nicholas II in Moscow hundreds of people were crushed to death in the Khodinka Fields.] I. Pavlovsky, the Paris correspondent of the *Novoye Vremya*, came with me to Melikhovo.

August 4. Opening of the school in Talezh. The peasants of Talezh, Bershov, Doubechnia and Sholkovo presented me with four loaves, an icon and two silver salt-cellars. The Sholkovo peasant Postnov made a speech.

N. stayed with me from the 15th to the 18th August. He has been forbidden [by the authorities] to publish anything: he speaks contemptuously now of the younger G., who said to the new Chief of the Central Press Bureau that he was not going to sacrifice his weekly *Nedelya* for N.'s sake and that "We have always anticipated the wishes of the Censorship." In fine weather N. walks in goloshes, and carries an umbrella, so as not to die of sunstroke; he is afraid to

[3]

wash in cold water, and complains of palpitations of the heart. From me he went on to L. N. Tolstoi.

I left Taganrog on August 24. In Rostov I had supper with a school-friend, L. Volkenstein, the barrister, who has already a house in town and a villa in Kislovodsk [in the Caucasus]. I was in Nakhichevan—what a change! All the streets are lit by electric light. In Kislovodsk, at the funeral of General Safonov, I met A. I. Tchouprov [a famous economist], later I met A. N. Vesselovsky [littérateur] in the park. On the 28th I went on a hunting party with Baron Steingel, passed the night in Bermamut. It was cold with a violent wind.

2 September in Novorissisk. Steamer *Alexander II*. On the 3rd I arrived at Feodossia and stopped with Souvorin. I saw I. K. Aivasovsky [famous painter] who said to me: "You no longer come to see me, an old man." In his opinion I ought to have paid him a visit. On the 16th in Kharkov, I was in the theatre at the performance of "The Dangers of Intelligence." 17th at home: wonderful weather.

Vladimir Sloviov [famous philosopher]

told me that he always carried an oak-gall in his trouser pocket,—in his opinion, it is a radical cure for piles.

October 17. Performance of my "Seagull" at the Alexandrinsky Theatre. It was not a success.

29th. I was at a meeting of the Zemstvo Council at Sezpukhovo.

On the 10th November I had a letter from A. F. Koni who says he liked my "Seagull" very much.

November 26th. A fire broke out in our house. Count S. I. Shakhovsky helped to put it out. When it was over, Sh. related that once, when a fire broke out in his house at night, he lifted a tank of water weighing 4½ cwt. and poured the water on the flames.

December 4. For the performance [of the "Seagull"] on the 17th October see "Theatral," No. 95, page 75. It is true that I fled from the theatre, but only when the play was over. In L.'s dressing-room during two or three acts. During the intervals there came to her officials of the State Theatres in uniform, wearing their orders, P. —with a Star; a handsome young official of the Department of the State Police also came to her. If a man takes up work which is alien to him, art for instance, then, since it is impossible for him to become an artist, he becomes an official. What a lot of people thus play the parasite round science, the theatre, the painting,—by putting on a uniform! Likewise the man to whom life is alien, who is incapable of living, nothing else remains for him, but to become an official. The fat actresses, who were in the dressing-room, made themselves pleasant to the officials—respectfully and flatteringly. (L. expressed her delight that P., so young, had already got the Star.) They were old, respectable house-keepers, serf-women, whom the masters honored with their presence.

December 21. Levitan suffers from dilation of the aorta. He carries clay on his chest. He has superb studies for pictures, and a passionate thirst for life.

December 31. P. I. Seryogin, the landscape painter, came.

1897.

From January 10 to February 3 busy with the census. I am enumerator of the 16th district, and have to instruct the other (fifteen) enumerators of our Bavykin Section. They all work superbly, except the priest of the Starospassky parish and the Government official, appointed to the Zemstvo, G., (who is in charge of the census district); he is away nearly all the time in Serpukhovo, spends every evening at the Club and keeps on wiring that he is not well. All the rest of the Government officials of our district are also said to do nothing.

With such critics as we have, authors like N. S. Lyeskov and S. V. Maximov cannot be a success.

Between "there is a God" and "there is no God" lies a whole vast tract, which the really wise man crosses with great effort. A Russian knows one or other of these two extremes, and the middle tract between them does not interest him; and therefore he usually knows nothing, or very little.

The ease with which Jews change their religion is justified by many on the ground of indifference. But this is not a justification. One has to respect even one's indifference, and not change it for anything, since indifference in a decent man is also a religion.

February 13. Dinner at Mme. Moros-ov's. Tchouprov, Sololevsky, Blaramberg, Sablin and myself were present.

February 15. Pancakes at Soldatien-kov's [a Moscow publisher]. Only Golziev [editor of *Russian Thought*] and myself were present. Many fine pictures, nearly all badly hung. After the pancakes we drove to Levitan, from whom Soldatienkov bought a picture and two studies for 1,100 roubles. Met Polyenov [famous painter]. In the evening I was at professor Ostrou-mov's; he says that Levitan "can't help dying." O. himself is ill and obviously frightened.

February 16. Several of us met in the ev-ening in the offices of *Russian Thought* to discuss the People's Theatre. Every one liked Shekhtel's plan.

February 19. Dinner at the "Continen-tal" to commemorate the great reform [the abolition of the serfdom in 1861]. Tedious and incongruous. To dine, drink cham-pagne, make a racket, and deliver speeches about national consciousness, the conscience of the people, freedom, and such things, while slaves in tail-coats are running round your

[8]

tables, veritable serfs, and your coachmen wait outside in the street, in the bitter cold—that is lying to the Holy Ghost.

February 22. I went to Serpukhovo to an amateur performance in aid of the school at Novossiolki. As far as Zarizin I was accompanied by. . . a little queen in exile,—an actress who imagines herself great; uneducated and a bit vulgar.

From March 25 till April 10 I was laid up in Ostroumov's clinic. Hæmorrhage. Creaking, moisture in the apices of both my lungs; congestion in the apex of the right. On March 28 L. N. Tolstoi came to see me. We spoke of immortality. I told him the gist of Nossilov's story "The Theatre of the Voguls," and he evidently listened with great pleasure.

May 1. N. arrived. He is always thanking you for tea and dinner, apologizing, afraid of being late for the train; he talks a great deal, keeps mentioning his wife, like Gogol's Mijniev, pushes the proofs of his play over to you, first one sheet then another, giggles, attacks Menshikov, whom Tolstoi has "swallowed"; assures you that he would shoot Stassiulevitch, if the latter were to

[9]

show himself at a review, as President of the Russian Republic; giggles again, wets his mustaches with the soup, eats hardly anything, and yet is quite a nice man after all.

May 4. The monks from the monastery paid us a visit. Dasha Moussin-Poushkin, the wife of the engineer Gliebov, who has been killed hunting, was there. She sang a great deal.

May 24. I was present at the examination of two schools in Tchirkov. [The Tchirkov and Mikhailovo schools.]

July 13. Opening of the school at Novossiolki which I have had built. The peasants gave me an icon with an inscription. The Zemstvo people were absent.

Braz [painter] does my portrait (for the Tretiakov Gallery). Two sittings a day.

July 22. I received a medal for my work on the census.

July 23. In Petersburg. Stopped at Souvorin's, in the drawing-room. Met VI. T. . . . who complained of his hysteria and praised his own books. I saw P. Gnyeditch and E. Karpov, who imitated Leykin showing off as a Spanish grandee.

July 27. At Leykin's at Ivanovsk. 28th

in Moscow. In the editorial offices of *Russian Thought*, bugs in the sofa.

September 4. Arrived in Paris. "Moulin Rouge," danse du ventre, Café du Néon with Coffins, Café du Ciel, etc.

September 8. In Biarritz. V. M. Sobolevsky and Mme. V. A. Morosov are here. Every Russian in Biarritz complains of the number of Russians here.

September 14. Bayonne. Grande course landoise. Bull-fight.

September 22. From Biarritz to Nice via Toulouse.

September 23. Nice. I settled into the Pension Russe. Met Maxim Kovalevsky; lunched at his house at Beaulieu, with N. I. Yurassov and Yakobi, the artist In Monte Carlo.

October 7. Confession of a spy.

October 9. I saw B.'s mother playing roulette. Unpleasant sight.

November 15. Monte Carlo. I saw how the croupier stole a louis d'or.

1898.

April 16. In Paris. Acquaintance with M. M. Antokolsky [sculptor] and negotiations for a statue of Peter the Great.

May 5. Returned home.

May 26. Sobolevsky came to Melikhovo. Must put down the fact that, in Paris, in spite of the rain and cold, I spent two or three weeks without being bored. Arrived here with M. Kovalevsky. Many interesting acquaintances: Paul Boyer, Art Roë, Bonnie, M. Dreyfus, De Roberti, Waliczewsky, Onieguin. Luncheons and dinners, at I. I. Schoukin's house. Left by Nord-express for Petersburg, whence to Moscow. At home, found wonderful weather.

An example of clerical boorishness. At a dinner party the critic Protopopov came up to M. Kovalevsky, clinked glasses and said: "I drink to science, so long as it does no harm to the people."

1901.

September 12. I was at L. Tolstoi's.

December 7. Talked to L. Tolstoi over the telephone.

1903.

January 8. "Istorichesky Vestnik," November 1902, "The Artistic Life of Moscow in the Seventies," by I. N. Zakharin. It is said in that article that I sent in my "Three Sisters" to the Theatrical and Literary Committee. It is not true.

ANTON CHEKHOV'S NOTE-BOOKS
(1892-1904)

MANKIND has conceived history as a series of battles; hitherto it has considered fighting as the main thing in life.

Solomon made a great mistake when he asked for wisdom.[1]

[1] Among Chekhov's papers the following monologue was found, written in his own hand:

Solomon (alone): Oh! how dark is life! No night, when I was a child, so terrified me by its darkness as does my invisible existence. Lord, to David my father thou gavest only the gift of harmonizing words and sounds, to sing and praise thee on strings, to lament sweetly, to make people weep or admire beauty; but why hast thou given me a meditative, sleepless, hungry mind? Like an insect born of the dust, I hide in darkness; and in fear and despair, all shaking and shivering, I see and hear in everything an invisible mystery. Why this morning? Why does the sun come out from behind the temple and gild the palm tree? Why this beauty of women? Where does the bird hurry, what is the meaning of its flight, if it and its young and the place to which it hastens will, like myself, turn to dust? It were better I had never been born or were a stone, to which God has given neither eyes nor thoughts. In order to tire out my body by nightfall, all day yesterday, like a mere workman I carried marble to the temple; but now the night has come and I cannot sleep . . . I'll go and lie down. Phorses told me that if one imagines a flock of sheep running and fixes one's attention upon it, the mind gets confused and one falls asleep. I'll do it. . . (exit).

[15]

Ordinary hypocrites pretend to be doves; political and literary hypocrites pretend to be eagles. But don't be disconcerted by their aquiline appearance. They are not eagles, but rats or dogs.

Those who are more stupid and more dirty than we are called the people. The administration classifies the population into taxpayers and non-taxpayers. But neither classification will do; we are all the people and all the best we are doing is the people's work.

If the Prince of Monaco has a roulette table, surely convicts may play at cards.

Iv. (Chekhov's brother Ivan) could philosophize about love, but he could not love.

Aliosha: "My mind, mother, is weakened by illness and I am now like a child: now I pray to God, now I cry, now I am happy."

Why did Hamlet trouble about ghosts after death, when life itself is haunted by ghosts so much more terrible?

[16]

Daughter: "Felt boots are not the correct thing."

Father: "Yes they are clumsy, I'll have to get leather ones." The father fell ill and his deportation to Siberia was postponed.

Daughter: "You are not at all ill, father. Look, you have your coat and boots on. . . ."

Father: "I long to be exiled to Siberia. One could sit somewhere by the Yenissey or Obi river and fish, and on the ferry there would be nice little convicts, emigrants. . . . Here I hate everything: this lilac tree in front of the window, these gravel paths. . . ."

A bedroom. The light of the moon shines so brightly through the window that even the buttons on his night shirt are visible.

A nice man would feel ashamed even before a dog. . . .

A certain Councillor of State, looking at a beautiful landscape, said: "What a marvelous function of nature!" From the note-book of an old dog: "People don't eat

[17]

slops and bones which the cooks throw away.
Fools!"

He had nothing in his soul except recollections of his schooldays.

The French say: "Laid comme un chenille"—as ugly as a caterpillar.

People are bachelors or old maids because they rouse no interest, not even a physical one.

The children growing up talked at meals about religion and laughed at fasts, monks, etc. The old mother at first lost her temper, then, evidently getting used to it, only smiled, but at last she told the children that they had convinced her, that she is now of their opinion. The children felt awkward and could not imagine what their old mother would do without her religion.

There is no national science, just as there is no national multiplication table; what is national is no longer science.

The dog walked in the street and was ashamed of its crooked legs.

The difference between man and woman: a woman, as she grows old gives herself up more and more to female affairs; a man, as he grows old, withdraws himself more and more from female affairs.

That sudden and ill-timed love-affair may be compared to this: you take boys somewhere for a walk; the walk is jolly and interesting—and suddenly one of them gorges himself with oil paint.

The character in the play says to every one: "You've got worms." He cures his daughter of the worms, and she turns yellow.

A scholar, without talent, a blockhead, worked for twenty-four years and produced nothing good, gave the world only scholars as untalented and as narrow-minded as himself. At night he secretly bound books— that was his true vocation: in that he was an artist and felt the joy of it. There came to him a bookbinder, who loved learning and studied secretly at night.

But perhaps the universe is suspended on the tooth of some monster.

Keep to the right, you of the yellow eye!

Do you want to eat?
No, on the contrary.

A pregnant woman with short arms and a long neck, like a kangaroo.

How pleasant it is to respect people! When I see books, I am not concerned with how the authors loved or played cards; I see only their marvelous works.

To demand that the woman one loves should be pure is egotistical: to look for that in a woman which I have not got myself is not love, but worship, since one ought to love one's equals.

The so-called pure childlike joy of life is animal joy.

A serious phlegmatic doctor fell in love with a girl who danced very well, and, to please her, he started to learn a mazurka.

The hen sparrow believes that her cock sparrow is not chirping but singing beautifully.

When one is peacefully at home, life seems ordinary, but as soon as one walks into the street and begins to observe, to question women, for instance, then life becomes terrible. The neighborhood of Patriarshi Prudy (a park and street in Moscow) looks quiet and peaceful, but in reality life there is hell.

These red-faced young and old women are so healthy that steam seems to exhale from them.

The estate will soon be brought under the hammer; there is poverty all round; and the footmen are still dressed like jesters.

There has been an increase not in the num-

[25]

ber of nervous diseases and nervous patients, but in the number of doctors able to study those diseases.

The more refined the more unhappy.

Life does not agree with philosophy: there is no happiness which is not idleness and only the useless is pleasurable.

The grandfather is given fish to eat, and if it does not poison him and he remains alive, then all the family eat it.

A correspondence. A young man dreams of devoting himself to literature and constantly writes to his father about it; at last he gives up the civil service, goes to Petersburg, and devotes himself to literature—he becomes a censor.

First class sleeping car. Passengers numbers 6, 7, 8 and 9. They discuss daughters-in-law. Simple people suffer from mothers-in-law, intellectuals from daughters-in-law. "My elder son's wife is educated, arranges Sunday schools and libraries, but she is tactless, cruel, capricious, and physically revolting. At dinner she will suddenly go off into sham hysterics because of some article in the newspaper. An affected thing." Another daughter-in-law: "In society she behaves passably, but at home she is a dolt, smokes, is miserly, and when she drinks tea, she keeps the sugar between her lips and teeth and speaks at the same time."

Miss Mieschankina.

In the servants' quarters Roman, a more or less dissolute peasant, thinks it his duty to look after the morals of the women servants.

A large fat barmaid—a cross between a pig and white sturgeon.

At Malo-Bronnaya (a street in Moscow). A little girl who has never been in the country feels it and raves about it, speaks about jackdaws, crows and colts, imagining parks and birds on trees.

Two young officers in stays.

A certain captain taught his daughter the art of fortification.

New literary forms always produce new forms of life and that is why they are so revolting to the conservative human mind.

A neurasthenic undergraduate comes home to a lonely country-house, reads French monologues, and finds them stupid.

People love talking of their diseases, although they are the most uninteresting things in their lives.

An official, who wore the portrait of the Governor's wife, lent money on interest; he secretly becomes rich. The late Governor's wife, whose portrait he has worn for fourteen years, now lives in a suburb, a poor widow; her son gets into trouble and she needs 4,000 roubles. She goes to the official, and he listens to her with a bored look and says: "I can't do anything for you, my lady."

Women deprived of the company of men

pine, men deprived of the company of women become stupid.

A sick innkeeper said to the doctor: "If I get ill, then for the love of God come without waiting for a summons. My sister will never call you in, whatever happens; she is a miser, and your fee is three roubles a visit." A month or two later the doctor heard that the innkeeper was seriously ill, and while he was making his preparations to go and see him, he received a letter from the sister saying: "My brother is dead." Five days later the doctor happened to go to the village and was told there that the innkeeper had died that morning. Disgusted he went to the inn. The sister dressed in black stood in the corner reading a psalm book. The doctor began to upbraid her for her stinginess and cruelty. The sister went on reading the psalms, but between every two sentences she stopped to quarrel with him—"Lots of your like running about here. . . . The devils brought you here." She belongs to the old faith, hates passionately and swears desperately.

[29]

The new governor made a speech to his
clerks. He called the merchants together—
another speech. At the annual prize-giving
of the secondary school for girls—a speech
on true enlightenment. To the representa-
tives of the press a speech. He called the
Jews together: "Jews, I have summoned
you.". . . A month or two passes—he does
nothing. Again he calls the merchants together—a speech. Again the Jews: "Jews,
I have summoned you.". . . He has wearied
them all. At last he says to his Chancellor:
"No, the work is too much for me, I shall
have to resign."

A student at a village theological school
was learning Latin by heart. Every half-
hour he runs down to the maids' room and,
closing his eyes, feels and pinches them; they
scream and giggle; he returns to his book
again. He calls it "refreshing oneself."

The Governor's wife invited an official,
who had a thin voice and was her adorer, to
have a cup of chocolate with her, and for a
week afterwards he was in bliss. He had
saved money and lent it but not on interest.

[30]

"I can't lend you any, your son-in-law would gamble it away. No, I can't." The son-in-law is the husband of the daughter who once sat in a box in a boa; he lost at cards and embezzled Government money. The official, who was accustomed to herring and vodka, and who had never before drunk chocolate, felt sick after the chocolate. The expression on the lady's face: "Aren't I a darling?"; she spent any amount of money on dresses and looked forward to making a display of them—so she gave parties.

Going to Paris with one's wife is like going to Tula [1] with one's samovar.

The young do not go in for literature, because the best of them work on steam engines, in factories, in industrial undertakings. All of them have now gone into industry, and industry is making enormous progress.

Families where the woman is bourgeoise easily breed adventurers, swindlers, and brutes without ideals.

[1] Tula is a Russian city where samovars are manufactured.

A professor's opinion: not Shakespeare, but the commentaries on him are the thing.

Let the coming generation attain happiness; but they surely ought to ask themselves, for what did their ancestors live and for what did they suffer.

Love, friendship, respect do not unite people as much as common hatred for something.

13th December. I saw the owner of a mill, the mother of a family, a rich Russian woman, who has never seen a lilac bush in Russia.

In a letter: "A Russian abroad, if not a spy, is a fool." The neighbor goes to Florence to cure himself of love, but at a distance his love grows stronger.

Yalta. A young man, interesting, liked by a lady of forty. He is indifferent to her, avoids her. She suffers and at last, out of spite, gets up a scandal about him.

Pete's mother even in her old age beaded her eyes.

Viciousness is a bag with which man is born.

B. said seriously that he is the Russian Maupassant.   And so did S.

A Jewish surname: Cap.

A lady looking like a fish standing on its head; her mouth like a slit, one longs to put a penny in it.

Russians abroad: the men love Russia passionately, but the women don't like her and soon forget her.

Chemist Propter.

Rosalie Ossipovna Aromat.

It is easier to ask of the poor than of the rich.

And she began to engage in prostitution,

got used to sleeping on the bed, while her aunt, fallen into poverty, used to lie on the little carpet by her side and jumped up each time the bell rang; when they left, she would say mindingly, with a pathetic grimace: "Something for the chamber-maid." And they would tip her sixpence.

Prostitutes in Monte Carlo, the whole tone is prostitutional; the palm trees, it seems, are prostitutes, and the chickens are prostitutes.

A big dolt, Z., a qualified nurse, of the Petersburg Rozhdestvensky School, having ideals, fell in love with X., a teacher, and believed him to be ideal, a public spirited worker after the manner of novels and stories of which she was so fond. Little by little she found him out, a drunkard, an idler, good-natured and not very clever. Dismissed, he began to live on his wife, sponged on her. He was an excrescence, a kind of sarcoma, who wasted her completely. She was once engaged to attend some intellectual country people, she went to them every day; they felt it awkward to give her money

—and, to her great vexation, gave her husband a suit as a present. He would drink tea for hours and this infuriated her. Living with her husband she grew thin, ugly, spiteful, stamped her foot and shouted at him: "Leave me, you low fellow." She hated him. She worked, and people paid the money to him, for, being a Zemstvo worker, she took no money, and it enraged her that their friends did not understand him and thought him ideal.

A young man made a million marks, lay down on them, and shot himself.

"That woman.". . . "I married when I was twenty; I have not drunk a glass of vodka all my life, haven't smoked a single cigarette." After he had run off with another woman, people got to like him more and to believe him more, and, when he walked in the street, he began to notice that they had all become kinder and nicer to him —because he had fallen.

A man and woman marry because both of them don't know what to do with themselves.

The power and salvation of a people lie in its intellegentsia, in the intellectuals who think honestly, feel, and can work.

A man without a mustache is like a woman with a mustache.

A man who cannot win a woman by a kiss will not win her by a blow.

For one sensible person there are a thousand fools, and for one sensible word there are a thousand stupid ones; the thousand overwhelms the one, and that is why cities and villages progress so slowly. The majority, the mass, always remain stupid; it will always overwhelm; the sensible man should give up hope of educating and lifting it up to himself; he had better call in the assistance of material force, build railways, telegraphs, telephones—in that way he will conquer and help life forward.

Really decent people are only to be found amongst men who have definite, either conservative or radical, convictions; so-called

[36]

moderate men are much inclined to rewards, commissions, orders, promotions.

"What did your uncle die of?"
"Instead of fifteen Botkin drops,[1] as the doctor prescribed, he took sixteen."

A young philologist, who has just left the University, comes home to his native town. He is elected churchwarden. He does not believe in God, but goes to church regularly, makes the sign of the cross when passing near a church or chapel, thinking that that sort of thing is necessary for the people and that the salvation of Russia is bound up with it. He is elected chairman of the Zemstvo board and a Justice of the Peace, he wins orders and medals; he does not notice that he has reached the age of forty-five; then suddenly he realizes that all the time he has been acting and making a fool of himself, but it is now too late to change his way of life. Once in his sleep he suddenly hears like the report of a gun the words: "What are you doing?"—and he starts up all in a sweat.

[1] A very harmless purgative.

[37]

One cannot resist evil, but one can resist good.

He flatters the authorities like a priest.

Instead of sheets—dirty tablecloths.

A Jewish surname: Perchik (little pepper).

A man in conversation: "And all the rest of it."

A rich man, usually insolent, his conceit enormous, but bears his riches like a cross. If the ladies and generals did not dispense charity on his account, if it were not for the poor students and the beggars, he would feel the anguish of loneliness. If the beggars struck and agreed not to beg from him, he would go to them himself.

The husband invites his friends to his country-house in the Crimea, and afterwards his wife, without her husband's knowledge, brings them the bill and is paid for board and lodging.

[38]

Potapov becomes attached to the brother, and this is the beginning of his falling in love with the sister. Divorces his wife. Afterwards the son sends him plans for a rabbit-hutch.

"I have sown clover and oats."
"No good; you had much better sow lucerne."
"I have begun to keep a pig."
"No good. It does not pay. You had better go in for mares."

A girl, a devoted friend, out of the best of motives, went about with a subscription list for X., who was not in want.

Why are the dogs of Constantinople so often described?

Disease: "He has got hydropathy."

I visit a friend, find him at supper; there are many guests. It is very gay; I am glad to chatter with the women and drink wine. A wonderfully pleasant mood. Suddenly up gets N. with an air of importance, as though he were a public prosecutor and makes a speech in my honor. "The magician of words . . . ideals . . . in our time when ideals grow dim . . . you are sowing wisdom, undying things. . . ." I feel as if I had had a cover over me and that now the cover had been taken off and some one was aiming a pistol at me.

After the speech—a murmur of conversation, then silence. The gayety has gone. "You must speak now," says my neighbor. But what can I say? I would gladly throw the bottle at him. And I go to bed with some sediment in my soul. "Look what a fool sits among you!"

The maid, when she makes the bed, always puts the slippers under the bed close to the wall. The fat master, unable to bear it any longer, gives the maid notice. It turns out that the doctor told her to put the slippers as far as possible under the bed so as to cure the man of his obesity.

The club blackballed a respectable man

because all of the members were out of humor; they ruined his prospects.

A large factory. The young employer plays the superior to all and is rude to the employees who have University degrees. Only the gardener, a German, has the courage to be offended: "How dare you, gold bag?"

A tiny little schoolboy with the name of Trachtenbauer.

Whenever he reads in the newspaper about the death of a great man, he wears mourning.

In the theatre. A gentleman asks a lady to take her hat off, as it is in his way. Grumbling, disagreeableness, entreaties. At last a confession: "Madam, I am the author of the play." She answered: "I don't care."

In order to act wisely it is not enough to be wise (Dostoevsky).

A. and B. have a bet. A. wins the wager,

by eating twelve cutlets; B. does not pay even for the cutlets.

It is terrible to dine every day with a person who stammers and says stupid things.

Glancing at a plump, appetizing woman: "It is not a woman, it is a full moon."

From her face one would imagine that under her stays she has got gills.

For a farce: Kapiton Ivanovitch Boil.

An income-tax inspector and an excise official, in order to justify their occupations to themselves, say spontaneously: "It is an interesting profession, there is a lot of work, it is a live occupation."

At twenty she loved Z., at twenty-four she married N. not because she loved him, but because she thought him a good, wise, ideal man. The couple lived happily; every one envies them, and indeed their life passes smoothly and placidly; she is satisfied, and, when people discuss love, she says that for

[42]

family life not love nor passion is wanted, but affection. But once the music played suddenly, and, inside her heart, everything broke up like ice in spring: she remembered Z. and her love for him, and she thought with despair that her life was ruined, spoilt for ever, and that she was unhappy. Then it happened to her with the New Year greetings; when people wished her "New Happiness," she indeed longed for new happiness.

Z. goes to a doctor, who examines him and finds that he is suffering from heart disease. Z. abruptly changes his way of life, takes medicine, can only talk about his disease; the whole town knows that he has heart disease and all the doctors, whom he regularly consults, say that he has got heart disease. He does not marry, gives up amateur theatricals, does not drink, and when he walks does so slowly and hardly breathes. Eleven years later he has to go to Moscow and there he consults a specialist. The latter finds that his heart is perfectly sound. Z. is overjoyed, but he can no longer return to a normal life, for he has got accustomed to going to bed early and to walking slowly, and he is bored if he cannot speak of his disease. The only result is that he gets to hate doctors—that is all.

A woman is fascinated not by art, but by the noise made by those who have to do with art.

N., a dramatic critic, has a mistress X., an actress. Her benefit night. The play is rotten, the acting poor, but N. has to praise. He writes briefly: "The play and the leading actress had an enormous success. Particulars to-morrow." As he wrote the last two words, he gave a sigh of relief. Next day he goes to X.; she opens the door, allows him to kiss and embrace her, and in a cutting tone says: "Particulars to-morrow."

In Kislovodsk or some other watering-place Z. picked up a girl of twenty-two; she was poor, straightforward, he took pity on her and, in addition to her fee, he left twenty-five roubles on the chest of drawers; he left her room with the feeling of a man who has done a good deed. The next time he visited her, he noticed an expensive ashtray and a man's fur cap, bought out of his twenty-five roubles—the girl again starving, her cheeks hollow.

N. mortgages his estate with the Bank of the Nobility at 4 per cent. and then lends the money on mortgage at 12 per cent.

Aristocrats? The same ugly bodies and physical uncleanliness, the same toothless old age and disgusting death, as with market-women.

N., when a group is being photographed, always stands in the front row; on addresses he always signs the first; at anniversaries he is always the first to speak. Always wonders: "O soup! O pastries!"

Z. got tired of having visitors, and he hired a French woman to live in his house as if she were his mistress. This shocked the ladies and he no longer had visitors.

Z. is a torch-bearer at funerals. He is an idealist. "In the undertaker's shop."

[45]

N. and Z. are intimate friends, but when they meet in society, they at once make fun of one another—out of shyness.

Complaint: "My son Stepan was delicate, and I therefore sent him to school in the Crimea, but there he was caned with a vine-branch, and that gave him philoxera in the behind and now the doctors can not cure him."

Mitya and Katya were told that their papa blasted rocks in the quarry. They wanted to blow up their cross grandpapa, so they took a pound of powder from their father's room, put it in a bottle, inserted a wick, and placed it under their grandfather's chair, when he was dozing after dinner; but soldiers marched by with the band playing— and this was the only thing that prevented them from carrying out their plan.

Sleep is a marvelous mystery of Nature which renews all the powers of man, bodily and spiritual. (Bishop Porphyrius Usgensky, "The Book of My Life.")

A woman imagines that she has a peculiar, exceptional constitution, whose ailments are different from other people's and which cannot stand ordinary medicine. She thinks that her son is unlike other people's sons, that he has to be brought up differently. She believes in principles, but she thinks that they apply to every one but herself, because she lives in exceptional circumstances. The son grows up, and she tries to find an exceptional wife for him. Those around her suffer. The son turns out a scoundrel.

Poor long-suffering art!

A man whose madness takes the form of an idea that he is a ghost: walks at night.

A sentimental man, like Lavrov, has moments of pleasant emotion and makes the request: "Write a letter to my auntie in Briansk; she is a darling. . . ."

There is a bad smell in the barn: ten years ago haymakers slept the night in it and ever since it smells.

[47]

An officer at a doctor's. The money on a plate. The doctor can see in the looking-glass that the patient takes twenty-five roubles from the plate and pays him with it.

Russia is a nobody's country!

Z. who is always saying banal things: "With the agility of a bear," "on one's favorite corn."

A savings bank: the clerk, a very nice man, looks down on the bank, considers it useless—and yet goes on working there.

A radical lady, who crosses herself at night, is secretly full of prejudice and superstition, hears that in order to be happy one should boil a black cat by night. She steals a cat and tries to boil it.

A publisher's twenty-fifth anniversary. Tears, a speech: "I offer ten roubles to the literary fund, the interest to be paid to the poorest writer, but on condition that a special committee is appointed to work out the rules according to which the distribution shall be made."

He wore a blouse and despised those who wore frock coats. A stew of trousers.

The ice cream is made of milk in which, as it were, the patients bathed.

It was a grand forest of timber, but a Government Conservator was appointed, and in two years time there was no more timber; the caterpillar pest.

X.: "Choleraic disorder in my stomach started with the cider."

Of some writers each work taken separately is brilliant, but taken as a whole they are indefinite; of others each particular work represents nothing outstanding; but, for all that, taken as a whole they are distinct and brilliant.

N. rings at the door of an actress; he is nervous, his heart beats, at the critical moment he gets into a panic and runs away; the

maid opens the door and sees nobody. He
returns, rings again—but has not the courage
to go in. In the end the porter comes out
and gives him a thrashing.

A gentle quiet schoolmistress secretly
beats her pupils, because she believes in the
good of corporal punishment.

N.: "Not only the dog, but even the
horses howled."

N. marries. His mother and sister see a
great many faults in his wife; they are distressed, and only after four or five years
realize that she is just like themselves.

The wife cried. The husband took her
by the shoulders and shook her, and she
stopped crying.

After his marriage everything—politics,
literature, society—did not seem to him as
interesting as they had before; but now
every trifle concerning his wife and child
became a most important matter.

"Why are thy songs so short?" a bird was once asked. "Is it because thou art short of breath?"

"I have very many songs and I should like to sing them all."

(A. Daudet.)

The dog hates the teacher; they tell it not to bark at him; it looks, does not bark, only whimpers with rage.

Faith is a spiritual faculty; animals have not got it; savages and uncivilized people have merely fear and doubt. Only highly developed natures can have faith.

Death is terrible, but still more terrible is the feeling that you might live for ever and never die.

The public really loves in art that which is banal and long familiar, that to which they have grown accustomed.

A progressive, educated, young, but stingy school guardian inspects the school every day, makes long speeches there, but does not spend a penny on it: the school is falling to pieces, but he considers himself useful and necessary. The teacher hates him, but he does not notice it. The harm is great. Once the teacher, unable to stand it any longer, facing him with anger and disgust, bursts out swearing at him.

Teacher: "Poushkin's centenary should not be celebrated; he did nothing for the church."

Miss Guitarov (actress).

If you wish to become an optimist and understand life, stop believing what people say and write, observe and discover for yourself.

Husband and wife zealously followed X.'s idea and built up their life according to it as if it were a formula. Only just before death they asked themselves: "Perhaps that idea is wrong? Perhaps the saying 'mens sana in corpore sano' is untrue?"

I detest: a playful Jew, a radical Ukrainian, and a drunken German.

The University brings out all abilities, including stupidity.

Taking into consideration, dear sir, as a result of this view, dear sir. . . .

The most intolerable people are provincial celebrities.

Owing to our flightiness, because the majority of us are unable and unaccustomed to think or to look deeply into life's phenomena, nowhere else do people so often say: "How banal!" nowhere else do people regard so superficially, and often contemptuously other people's merits or serious questions. On the other hand nowhere else does the authority of a name weigh so heavily as with us Russians, who have been abased by centuries of slavery and fear freedom. . .

A doctor advised a merchant to eat soup and chicken. The merchant thought the advice ironical. At first he ate a dinner of

[53]

botvinia and pork, and then, as if recollecting the doctor's orders, ordered soup and chicken and swallowed them down too, thinking it a great joke.

Father Epaminond catches fish and puts them in his pocket; then, when he gets home, he takes out a fish at a time, as he wants it, and fries it.

The nobleman X. sold his estate to N. with all the furniture according to an inventory, but he took away everything else, even the oven dampers, and after that N. hated all noblemen.

The rich, intellectual X., of peasant origin, implored his son: "Mike, don't get out of your class. Be a peasant until you die, do not become a nobleman, nor a merchant, nor a bourgeois. If, as you say, the Zemstvo officer now has the right to inflict corporal punishment on peasants, then let him also have the right to punish you." He was proud of his peasant origin, he was even haughty about it.

[54]

They celebrated the birthday of an honest man. Took the opportunity to show off and praise one another. Only towards the end of the dinner they suddenly discovered that the man had not been invited; they had forgotten.

A gentle quiet woman, getting into a temper, says: "If I were a man, I would just bash your filthy mug."

A Mussulman for the salvation of his soul digs a well. It would be a pleasant thing if each of us left a school, a well, or something like that, so that life should not pass away into eternity without leaving a trace behind it.

We are tired out by servility and hypocrisy.

N. once had his clothes torn by dogs, and now, when he pays a call anywhere, he asks: "Aren't there any dogs here?"

A young pimp, in order to keep up his powers, always eats garlic.

School guardian. Widowed priest plays the harmonium and sings: "Rest with the saints."

In July the red bird sings the whole morning.

"A large selection of *cigs*" [1] —so read X. every day when he went down the street, and wondered how one could deal only in *cigs* and who wanted them. It took him thirty years before he read it correctly: "A large selection of cigars."

A bride to an engineer: a dynamite cartridge filled with one-hundred-rouble notes.

"I have not read Herbert Spencer. Tell me his subjects. What does he write about?" "I want to paint a panel for the Paris exhibition. Suggest a subject." (A wearisome lady.)

The idle, so-called governing, classes cannot remain long without war. When there

[1] *Cigs* in Russian is a kind of fish.

is no war they are bored, idleness fatigues and irritates them, they do not know what they live for; they bite one another, try to say unpleasant things to one another, if possible with impunity, and the best of them make the greatest efforts not to bore the others and themselves. But when war comes, it possesses all, takes hold of the imagination, and the common misfortune unites all.

An unfaithful wife is a large cold cutlet which one does not want to touch, because some one else has had it in his hands.

An old maid writes a treatise: "The tram-line of piety."

Ryzeborsky, Tovbin, Gremoukhin, Koptin.

She had not sufficient skin on her face; in order to open her eyes she had to shut her mouth and *vice versa*.

When she raises her skirt and shows her lace petticoat, it is obvious that she dresses like a woman who is accustomed to be seen by men.

X. philosophizes: "Take the word 'nose.' In Russia it seems something unmentionable, means the deuce knows what, one may say, the indecent part of the body, and in French it means wedding." And indeed X.'s nose was an indecent part of the body.

A girl, flirting, chatters: "All are afraid of me . . . men, and the wind . . . ah, leave me alone! I shall never marry." And at home poverty, her father a regular drunkard. And if people could see how she and her mother work, how she screens her father, they would feel the deepest respect for her and would wonder why she is so ashamed of poverty and work, and is not ashamed of that chatter.

A restaurant. An advanced conversation. Andrey Andreyevitch, a good-natured bourgeois, suddenly declares: "Do you know, gentlemen, I was once an anarchist!" Every one is astonished. A. A. tells the following tale: a strict father; a technical

[58]

school opened in the provincial town in a craze for technical education; they have no ideas and they did not know what to teach (since, if you are going to make shoemakers of all the inhabitants, who will buy the shoes?); he was expelled and his father turned him out of the house; he had to take a job as an assistant clerk on the squire's estate; he became enraged with the rich, the well-fed, and the fat; the squire planted cherry trees, A. A. helped him, and suddenly a desire came over him to cut off the squire's white fat fingers with the spade, as if it were by accident; and closing his eyes he struck a blow with the shovel as hard as he could, but it missed. Then he went away; the forest, the quiet in the fields, rain; he longed for warmth, went to his aunt, she gave him tea and rolls—and his anarchism was gone. After the story there passed by the table Councillor of State L. Immediately A. A. gets up and explains how L., Councillor of State, owns houses, etc.

I was apprenticed to a tailor. He cut the trousers; I did the sewing, but the stripe came down here right over the knee. Then I was apprenticed to a cabinet-maker. I

[59]

was planing once when the plane flew out of my hands and hit the window; it broke the glass. The squire was a Lett, his name Shtoppev [1]; and he had an expression on his face as if he were going to wink and say: "Wouldn't it be nice to have a drink?" In the evenings he drank, drank by himself—and I felt hurt.

A dealer in cider puts labels on his bottles with a crown printed on them. It irritates and vexes X. who torments himself with the idea that a mere trader is usurping the crown. X. complains to the authorities, worries every one, seeks redress and so on; he dies from irritation and worry.

A governess is teased with the nickname Gesticulation.

Shaptcherigin, Zambisebulsky, Sveentchutka, Chemburaklya.

Senile pomposity, senile vindictiveness. What a number of despicable old men I have known!

[1] *Shtopov* means "cork-screw."

[60]

How delightful when on a bright frosty morning a new sleigh with a rug comes to the door.

X. arrived to take up duty at N., he shows himself a despot: he is annoyed when some one else is a success; he becomes quite different in the presence of a third person; when a woman is present, his tone changes; when he pours out wine, he first puts a little in his own glass and then helps the company; when he walks with a lady he takes her arm; in general he tries to show refinement. He does not laugh at other people's jokes: "You repeat yourself." "There is nothing new in that." Every one is sick of him; he sermonizes. The old women nickname him "the top."

A man who can not do anything, does not know how to act, how to enter a room, how to ask for anything.

Utiujnᵛ

A man who always insists: "I haven't

got syphilis. I'm an honest man. My wife is an honest woman."

X. all his life spoke and wrote about the vices of servants and about the way to manage and control them, and he died deserted by every one except his valet and his cook.

A little girl with rapture about her aunt: "She is very beautiful, as beautiful as our dog!"

Marie Ivanovna Kolstovkin.

In a love letter: "Stamp enclosed for a reply."

The best men leave the villages for the towns, and therefore the villages decline and will continue to decline.

Pavel was a cook for forty years; he loathed the things which he cooked and he never ate.

He ceased to love a woman; the sensation

of not being in love; a peaceful state of mind; long peaceful thoughts.

Conservative people do so little harm because they are timid and have no confidence in themselves; harm is done not by conservative but by malicious people.

One of two things: either sit in the carriage or get out of it.

For a play: an old woman of radical views dresses like a girl, smokes, cannot exist without company, sympathetic.

In a Pullman car—these are the dregs of society.

On the lady's bosom was the portrait of a fat German.

A man who at all elections all his life long always voted against the Left.

They undressed the corpse, but had no time to take the gloves off; a corpse in gloves.

[63]

A farmer at dinner boasts: "Life in the country is cheap—one has one's own chickens, one's own pigs—life is cheap."

A customs official, from want of love for his work, searches the passengers, looking for documents of a suspicious political nature, and makes even the gendarmes indignant.

A real male (mouzhtchina) consists of man (mouzh) and title (tchin).

Education: "Masticate your food properly," their father told them. And they masticated properly, and walked two hours every day, and washed in cold water, and yet they turned out unhappy and without talent.

Commercial and industrial medicine.

N. forty years old married a girl seventeen. The first night, when they returned to his mining village, she went to bed and suddenly burst into tears, because she did not love him. He is a good soul, is overwhelmed with distress, and goes off to sleep in his little working room.

On the spot where the former manor house stood there is no trace left; only one lilac bush remains and that for some reason does not bloom.

Son: "To-day I believe is Thursday."
Mother: (not having heard) "What?"
Son: (angrily) "Thursday!" (quietly) "I ought to take a bath."
Mother: "What?"
Son: (angry and offended) "Bath!"

N. goes to X. every day, talks to him, and shows real sympathy in his grief; suddenly X. leaves his house, where he was so comfortable. N. asks X.'s mother why he went away. She answers: "Because you came to see him every day."

It was such a romantic wedding, and later —what fools! what babies!

Love. Either it is a remnant of something degenerating, something which once has been immense, or it is a particle of what will in the future develop into something immense; but in the present it is unsatisfying, it gives much less than one expects.

A very intellectual man all his life tells lies about hypnotism, spiritualism—and people believe him; yet he is quite a nice man.

In Act I, X., a respectable man, borrows a hundred roubles from N., and in the course of all four acts he does not pay it back.

A grandmother has six sons and three daughters, and best of all she loves the failure, who drinks and has been in prison.

N., the manager of a factory, rich, with a wife and children, happy, has written "An investigation into the mineral spring at X." He was much praised for it and was invited to join the staff of a newspaper; he gave up his post, went to Petersburg, divorced his wife, spent his money—and went to the dogs.

(Looking at a photograph album):
"Whose ugly face is that?"
"That's my uncle."

Alas, what is terrible is not the skeletons,
but the fact that I am no longer terrified by
them.

A boy of good family, capricious, full of
mischief, obstinate, wore out his whole family. The father, an official who played the
piano, got to hate him, took him into a corner of the garden, flogged him with consid-
erable pleasure, and then felt disgusted with
himself. The son has grown up and is an
officer.

N. courted Z. for a long time. She was
very religious, and, when he proposed to her,
she put a dried flower, which he had once
given to her, into her prayer-book.

Z: "As you are going to town, post my
letter in the letter-box."
N: (alarmed) "Where? I don't know
where the letter-box is."

[67]

Z: "Will you also call at the chemist's and get me some naphthaline?"

N: (alarmed) "I'll forget the naphthaline, I'll forget."

A storm at sea. Lawyers ought to regard it as a crime.

X. went to stay with his friend in the country. The place was magnificent, but the servants treated him badly, he was uncomfortable, although his friend considered him a big man. The bed was hard, he was not provided with a night shirt and he felt ashamed to ask for one.

At a rehearsal. The wife:
"How does that melody in Pagliacci go? Whistle it."
"One must not whistle on the stage; the stage is a temple."

He died from fear of cholera.

As like as a nail is to a requiem.

A conversation on another planet about

the earth a thousand years hence. "Do you remember that white tree?"

Anakhthema!

Zigzagovsky, Oslizin, Svintchulka, Derbaliguin.

A woman with money, the money hidden everywhere, in her bosom and between her legs. . . .

All that procedure.

Treat your dismissal as you would an atmospheric phenomenon.

A conversation at a conference of doctors. First doctor: "All diseases can be cured by salt." Second doctor, military: "Every disease can be cured by prescribing no salt." The first points to his wife, the second to his daughter.

The mother has ideals, the father too; they delivered lectures; they built schools, museums, etc. They grow rich. And their children are most ordinary; spend money, gamble on the Stock Exchange.

N. married a German when she was seventeen. He took her to live in Berlin. At forty she became a widow and by that time spoke Russian badly and German badly.

The husband and wife loved having visitors, because, when there were no visitors they quarreled.

It is an absurdity! It is an anachronism!

"Shut the window! You are perspiring! Put on an overcoat! Put on goloshes!"

If you wish to have little spare time, do nothing.

On a Sunday morning in summer is heard the rumble of a carriage—people driving to mass.

For the first time in her life a man kissed

her hand; it was too much for her, it turned her head.

What wonderful names: the little tears of Our Lady, warbler, crows-eyes.[1]

A government forest officer with shoulder straps, who has never seen a forest.

A gentleman owns a villa near Mentone; he bought it out of the proceeds of the sale of his estate in the Tula province. I saw him in Kharkhov to which he had come on business; he gambled away the villa at cards and became a railway clerk; after that he died.

At supper he noticed a pretty woman and choked; a little later he caught sight of another pretty woman and choked again, so that he did not eat his supper—there were a lot of pretty women.

A doctor, recently qualified, supervises the food in a restaurant. "The food is under

---

[1] The names of flowers.

the special supervision of a doctor." He copies out the chemical composition of the mineral water; the students believe him— and all is well.

He did not eat, he partook of food.

A man, married to an actress, during a performance of a play in which his wife was acting, sat in a box, with beaming face, and from time to time got up and bowed to the audience.

Dinner at Count O. D.'s. Fat lazy footmen; tasteless cutlets; a feeling that a lot of money is being spent, that the situation is hopeless, and that it is impossible to change the course of things.

A district doctor: "What other damned creature but a doctor would have to go out in such weather?"—he is proud of it, grumbles about it to every one, and is proud to think that his work is so troublesome; he does not drink and often sends articles to medical journals that do not publish them.

When N. married her husband, he was junior Public Prosecutor; he became judge of the High Court and then judge of the Court of Appeals; he is an average uninteresting man. N. loves her husband very much. She loves him to the grave, writes him meek and touching letters when she hears of his unfaithfulness, and dies with a touching expression of love on her lips. Evidently she loved, not her husband, but some one else, superior, beautiful, non-existent, and she lavished that love upon her husband. And after her death footsteps could be heard in her house.

They are members of a temperance society and now and again take a glass of wine.

They say: "In the long run truth will triumph;" but it is untrue.

A clever man says: "This is a lie, but since the people can not do without the lie, since it has the sanction of history, it is dangerous to root it out all at once; let it go on for the time being but with certain corrections."

But the genius says: "This is a lie, therefore it must not exist."

Marie Ivanovna Kladovaya.

A schoolboy with mustaches, in order to show off, limps with one leg.

A writer of no talent, who has been writing for a long time, with his air of importance reminds one of a high priest.

Mr. N. and Miss Z. in the city of X. Both clever, educated, of radical views, and both working for the good of their fellow men, but both hardly know each other and in conversation always rail at each other in order to please the stupid and coarse crowd.

He flourished his hand as if he were going to seize him by the hair and said: "You won't escape by that there trick."

N. has never been in the country and thinks that in the winter country people use skis. "How I would enjoy ski-ing now!"

Madam N., who sells herself, says to each man who has her: "I love you because you are not like the rest."

An intellectual woman, or rather a woman who belongs to an intellectual circle, excels in deceit.

N. struggled all his life investigating a disease and studying its bacilli; he devoted his whole life to the struggle, expended on it all his powers, and suddenly just before his death it turned out that the disease is not in the least infectious or dangerous.

A theatrical manager, lying in bed, read a new play. He read three or four pages and then in irritation threw the play on to the floor, put out the candle, and drew the bed-clothes over him; a little later, after thinking over it, he took the play up again and began to read it; then, getting angry with the uninspired tedious work, he again threw it on the floor and put out the candle. A little later he once more took up the play and read it, then he produced it and it was a failure.

[75]

N., heavy, morose, gloomy, says: "I love a joke, I am always joking."

The wife writes; the husband does not like her writing, but out of delicacy says nothing and suffers all his life.

The fate of an actress: the beginning—a well-to-do family in Kertch, life dull and empty; the stage, virtue, passionate love, then lovers; the end: unsuccessful attempt to poison herself, then Kertch, life at her fat uncle's house, the delight of being left alone. Experience shows that an artist must dispense with wine, marriage, pregnancy. The stage will become art only in the future, now it is only struggling for the future.

(Angrily and sententiously) "Why don't you give me your wife's letters to read? Aren't we relations?"

Lord, don't allow me to condemn or to speak of what I do not know or do not understand.

Why do people describe only the weak,

surly and frail as sinners? And every one
when he advises others to describe only the
strong, healthy, and interesting, means himself.

For a play: a character always lying without rhyme or reason.

Sexton Catacombov.

N. N., a litterateur, critic, plausible, self-
confident, very liberal minded, talks about
poetry; condescendingly agrees with one—
and I see that he is a man absolutely without
talent (I haven't read him). Some one
suggests going to Ai-Petri. I say that it is
going to rain, but we set out. The road is
muddy, it rains; the critic sits next to me, I
feel his lack of talent. He is wooed and
made a fuss of as if he were a bishop. And
when it cleared up, I went back on foot.
How easily people deceive themselves, how
they love prophets and soothsayers; what a
herd it is! Another person went with us, a
Councillor of State, middle-aged, silent because he thinks he is right and despises the
critic, because he too is without talent. A

girl afraid to smile because she is among clever people.

Alexey Ivanitch Prokhladitelny (refreshing) or Doushespasitelny (soul-saving). A girl: "I would marry him, but am afraid of the name—Madam Refreshing."

A dream of a keeper in the zoölogical gardens. He dreams that there was presented to the Zoo first a marmot, then an emu, then a vulture, then a she-goat, then another emu; the presentations are made without end and the Zoo is crowded out—the keeper wakes up in horror wet with perspiration.

"To harness slowly but drive rapidly is in the nature of this people," said Bismarck.

When an actor has money, he doesn't send letters but telegrams.

With insects, out of the caterpillar comes the butterfly; with mankind it is the other way round, out of the butterfly comes the caterpillar.[1]

[1]There is a play on words here, the Russian word for butterfly also means a woman.

[78]

The dogs in the house became attached not to their masters who fed and fondled them, but to the cook, a foreigner, who beat them.

Sophie was afraid that her dog might catch cold, because of the draught.

The soil is so good, that, were you to plant a shaft, in a year's time a cart would grow out of it.

X. and Z., very well educated and of radical views, married. In the evening they talked together pleasantly, then quarreled, then came to blows. In the morning both are ashamed and surprised, they think that it must have been the result of some exceptional state of their nerves. Next night again a quarrel and blows. And so every night until at last they realize that they are not at all educated, but savage, just like the majority of people.

A play: in order to avoid having visitors, Z. pretends to be a regular tippler, although he drinks nothing.

When children appear on the scene, then we justify all our weaknesses, our compromises, and our snobbery, by saying: "It's for the children's sake."

Count, I am going away to Mordegundia. (A land of horrible faces.)

Barbara Nedotyopin.

Z., an engineer or doctor, went on a visit to his uncle, an editor; he became interested, began to go there frequently; then became a contributor to the paper, little by little gave up his profession; one night he came out of the newspaper office, remembered, and seized his head in his hands—"all is lost!" He began to go gray. Then it became a habit, he was quite white now and flabby, an editor, respectable but obscure.

A Privy Councillor, an old man, looking at his children, became a radical himself.

A newspaper: "Cracknel."

The clown in the circus—that is talent, and the waiter in the frock coat speaking to him—that is the crowd; the waiter with an ironical smile on his face.

Auntie from Novozybkov.

He has a rarefaction of the brain and his brains have leaked into his ears.

"What? Writers? If you like, for a shilling I'll make a writer of you."

Instead of translator, contractor.

An actress, forty years old, ugly, ate a partridge for dinner, and I felt sorry for the partridge, for it occurred to me that in its life it had been more talented, more sensible, and more honest than that actress.

The doctor said to me: "If," says he, "your constitution holds out, drink to your heart's content." (Gorbunov.)

Carl Kremertartarlau.

[81]

A field with a distant view, one tiny birch tree. The inscription under the picture: loneliness.

The guests had gone: they had played cards and everything was in disorder: tobacco smoke, scraps of paper, and chiefly—the dawn and memories.

Better to perish from fools than to accept praises from them.

Why do trees grow and so luxuriantly, when the owners are dead?

The character keeps a library, but he is always away visiting; there are no readers.

Life seems great, enormous, and yet one sits on one's *piatachok*. [1]

Zolotonosha? [2] There is no such town! No!

---

[1] The word means five kopecks and also a pig's snout.
[2] The name of a Russian town, meaning literally "Gold-carrier."

When he laughs, he shows his teeth and gums.

He loved the sort of literature which did not upset him, Schiller, Homer, etc.

N., a teacher, on her way home in the evening was told by her friend that X. had fallen in love with her, N., and wanted to propose. N., ungainly, who had never before thought of marriage, when she got home, sat for a long time trembling with fear, could not sleep, cried, and towards morning fell in love with X.; next day she heard that the whole thing was a supposition on the part of her friend and that X. was going to marry not her but Y.

He had a liaison with a woman of forty-five after which he began to write ghost stories.

I dreamt that I was in India and that one of the local princes presented me with an elephant, two elephants even. I was so worried about the elephant that I woke up.

An old man of eighty says to another old man of sixty: "You ought to be ashamed, young man."

When they sang in church, "Now is the beginning of our salvation," he ate *glavizna* at home; on the day of St. John the Baptist he ate no food that was circular and flogged his children.[1]

A journalist wrote lies in the newspaper, but he thought he was writing the truth.

If you are afraid of loneliness, do not marry.

He himself is rich, but his mother is in the workhouse.

He married, furnished a house, bought a writing-table, got everything in order, but found he had nothing to write.

[1] *Glavizna* in Russian is the name of a fish and also means beginning; the root of the verbs "to behead" and "to flog" are the same.

Faust: "What you don't know is just what you want; what you know is what you can't use."

Although you may tell lies, people will believe you, if only you speak with authority.

As I shall lie in the grave alone, so in fact I live alone.

A German: "Lord have mercy on us, *grieshniki.*" [1]

"O my dear little pimple!" said the bride tenderly. The bridegroom thought for a while, then felt hurt—they parted.

They were mineral water bottles with preserved cherries in them.

An actress who spoilt all her parts by very bad acting— and this continued all her life long until she died. Nobody liked

[1] *Grieshniki* means "sinners," but sounds like *grietchnieviki* which means "buckwheat cakes."

[85]

her; she ruined all the best parts; and yet she went on acting until she was seventy.

He alone is all right and can repent who feels himself to be wrong.

The archdeacon curses the "doubters," and they stand in the choir and sing anathema to themselves (Skitalez).

He imagined that his wife lay with her legs cut off and that he nursed her in order to save his soul. . . .

Madame Snuffley.

The black-beetles have left the house; the house will be burnt down.

"Dmitri, the Pretender, and Actors." "Turgenev and the Tigers." Articles like that can be and are written.

A title: Lemon Peel.

I am your legitimate husband.

An abortion, because while bathing a wave struck her, a wave of the ocean; because of the eruption of Vesuvius.

It seems to me: the sea and myself—and nothing else.

Education: his three-year-old son wore a black frock-coat, boots, and waistcoat.

With pride: "I'm not of Yuriev, but of Dorpat University." [1]

His beard looked like the tail of a fish.

A Jew, Ziptchik.

A girl, when she giggles, makes noises as if she were putting her head in cold water.

"Mamma, what is a thunderbolt made of?"

On the estate there is a bad smell, and bad taste; the trees are planted anyhow,

[1] Yuriev is the Russian name of the town Dorpat.

[87]

stupidly; and away in a remote corner the lodge-keeper's wife all day long washes the guest's linen—and nobody sees her; and the owners are allowed to talk away whole days about their rights and their nobility.

She fed her dog on the best caviare.

Our self-esteem and conceit are European, but our culture and actions are Asiatic.

A black dog—he looks as if he were wearing goloshes.

A Russian's only hope—to win two hundred thousand roubles in a lottery.

She is wicked, but she taught her children good.

Every one has something to hide.

The title of N.'s story: The Power of Harmonies.

O how nice it would be if bachelors or widowers were appointed Governors.

A Moscow actress never in her life saw a turkey-hen.

On the lips of the old I hear either stupidity or malice.

"Mamma, Pete did not say his prayers." Pete is woken up, he says his prayers, cries, then lies down and shakes his fist at the child who made the complaint.

He imagined that only doctors could say whether it is male or female.

One became a priest, the other a *Dukhobor*, the third a philosopher, and in each case instinctively because no one wants really to work with bent back from morning to night.

A passion for the word uterine: my uterine brother, my uterine wife, my uterine brother-in-law, etc.

To Doctor N., an illegitimate child, who has never lived with his father and knew him very little, his bosom friend Z., says with agitation: "You see, the fact of the matter is that your father misses you very much, he is ill and wants to have a look at you." The father keeps "Switzerland," furnished apartments. He takes the fried fish out of the dish with his hands and only afterwards uses a fork. The vodka smells rank. N. went, looked about him, had dinner—his only feeling that that fat peasant, with the grizzled beard, should sell such filth. But once, when passing the house at midnight, he looked in at the window: his father was sitting with bent back reading a book. He recognized himself and his own manners.

As stupid as a gray gelding.

They teased the girl with castor oil, and therefore she did not marry.

N. all his life used to write abusive letters to famous singers, actors, and authors: "You think, you scamp, . . ."—without signing his name.

When the man who carried the torch at funerals came out in his three-cornered hat, his frock coat with laces and stripes, she fell in love with him.

A sparkling, joyous nature, a kind of living protest against grumblers; he is fat and healthy, eats a great deal, every one likes him but only because they are afraid of the grumblers; he is a nobody, a Ham, only eats and laughs loud, and that's all; when he dies, every one sees that he had done nothing, that they had mistaken him for some one else.

After the inspection of the building, the Commission, which was bribed, lunched heartily, and it was precisely a funeral feast over honesty.

He who tells lies is dirty.

At three o'clock in the morning they wake him: he has to go to his job at the railway station, and so every day for the last fourteen years.

A lady grumbles: "I write to my son that he should change his linen every Saturday.

He replies: 'Why Saturday, not Monday?'
I answer: 'Well, all right, let it be Monday.'
And he: 'Why Monday, not Tuesday?' He
is a nice honest man, but I get worried by
him."

A clever man loves learning but is a fool
at teaching.

The sermons of priests, archimandrites,
and bishops are wonderfully like one another.

One remembers the arguments about the
brotherhood of man, public good, and work
for the people, but really there were no such
arguments, one only drank at the University.
They write: "One feels ashamed of the men
with University degrees who once fought
for human rights and freedon of religion and
conscience"—but they never fought.

Every day after dinner the husband
threatens his wife that he will become a
monk, and the wife cries.

Mordokhvostov.

Husband and wife have lived together and quarreled for eighteen years. At last he makes a confession, which was in fact untrue, of having been false to her, and they part to his great pleasure and to the wrath of the whole town.

A useless thing, an album with forgotten, uninteresting photographs, lies in the corner on a chair; it has been lying there for the last twenty years and no one makes up his mind to throw it away.

N. tells how forty years ago X., a wonderful and extraordinary man, had saved the lives of five people, and N. feels it strange that every one listened with indifference, that the history of X. is already forgotten, uninteresting. . . .

They fell upon the soft caviare greedily, and devoured it in a minute.

In the middle of a serious conversation he says to his little son: "Button up your trousers."

[93]

Man will only become better when you make him see what he is like.

Dove-colored face.

The squire feeds his pigeons, canaries, and fowls on pepper, acids, and all kinds of rubbish in order that the birds may change their color—and that is his sole occupation: he boasts of it to every visitor.

They invited a famous singer to recite the Acts of the Apostles at the wedding; he recited it, but they have not paid his fee.

For a farce: I have a friend by name Krivomordy (crooked face) and he's all right. Not crooked leg or crooked arm but crooked face: he was married and his wife loved him.

N. drank milk every day, and every time he put a fly in the glass and then, with the air of a victim, asked the old butler: "What's that?" He could not live a single day without that.

She is surly and smells of a vapor bath.

N. learned of his wife's adultery. He is indignant, distressed, but hesitates and keeps silent. He keeps silence and ends by borrowing money from Z., the lover, and continues to consider himself an honest man.

When I stop drinking tea and eating bread and butter, I say: "I have had enough." But when I stop reading poems or novels, I say: "No more of that, no more of that."

A solicitor lends money at a high rate of interest, and justifies himself because he is leaving everything to the University of Moscow.

A little sexton, with radical views: "Nowadays our fellows crawl out from all sorts of unexpected holes."

The squire N. always quarrels with his neighbors who are Molokans [1]; he goes to court, abuses and curses them; but when at

1 Molokans are a religious sect in Russia.

last they leave, he feels there is an empty place; he ages rapidly and pines away.

Mordukhanov.

With N. and his wife there lives the wife's brother, a lachrymose young man who at one time steals, at another tells lies, at another attempts suicide; N. and his wife do not know what to do, they are afraid to turn him out because he might kill himself; they would like to turn him out, but they do not know how to manage it. For forging a bill he gets into prison, and N. and his wife feel that they are to blame; they cry, grieve. She died from grief; he too died some time later and everything was left to the brother who squandered it and got into prison again.

Suppose I had to marry a woman and live in her house, I would run away in two days, but a woman gets used so quickly to her husband's house, as though she had been born there.

Well, you are a Councillor; but whom do you counsel? God forbid that any one should listen to your counsels.

The little town of Torjok. A sitting of the town council. Subject: the raising of the rates. Decision: to invite the Pope to settle down in Torjok—to choose it as his residence.

S.'s logic: I am for religious toleration, but against religious freedom; one cannot allow what is not in the strict sense orthodox.

St. Piony and Epinach. ii March, Pupli 13 m.

Poetry and works of art contain not what is needed but what people desire; they do not go further than the crowd and they express only what the best in the crowd desire.

A little man is very cautious; he sends even letters of congratulation by registered post in order to get a receipt.

[97]

Russia is an enormous plain across which wander mischievous men.

Platonida Ivanovna.

If you are politically sound, that is enough for you to be considered a perfectly satisfactory citizen; the same thing with radicals, to be politically unsound is enough, everything else will be ignored.

A man who when he fails opens his eyes wide.

Ziuzikov.

A Councillor of State, a respectable man; it suddenly comes out that he has secretly kept a brothel.

N. has written a good play; no one praises him or is pleased; they all say: "We'll see what you write next."

The more important people came in by

the front door, the simple folk by the back door.

He: "And in our town there lived a man whose name was Kishmísh (raisin). He called himself Kíshmish, but every one knew that he was Kishmísh."

She (after some thought): "How annoying . . . if only his name had been Sultana, but Kíshmish! . . ."

Blagovospitanny.

Most honored Iv-Iv-itch!

How intolerable people are sometimes who are happy and successful in everything.

They begin gossiping that N. is living with Z.; little by little an atmosphere is created in which a liaison of N. and Z. becomes inevitable.

When the locust was a plague, I wrote against the locust and enchanted every one, I was rich and famous; but now, when the locust has long ago disappeared and is forgotten, I am merged in the crowd, forgotten, and not wanted.

Merrily, joyfully: "I have the honor to introduce you to Iv. Iv. Izgoyev, my wife's lover."

Everywhere on the estate are notices: "Trespassers will be prosecuted," "Keep off the flowers," etc.

In the great house is a fine library which is talked about but is never used; they give you watery coffee which you cannot drink; the garden is tasteless with no flowers in it —and they pretend that all this is something Tolstoian.

He learnt Swedish in order to study Ibsen, spent a lot of time and trouble, and suddenly realized that Ibsen is not important; he could not conceive what use he could now make of the Swedish language. [1]

[1] Ibsen wrote in Norwegian of course. Responding to a request for his interpretation of this curious paragraph. Mr. Koteliansky writes:
"Chekhov had a very high opinion of Ibsen; the

N. makes a living by exterminating bugs; and for the purposes of his trade he reads the works of——. If in "The Cossacks," bugs are not mentioned, it means that "The Cossacks" is a bad book.

Man is what he believes.

A clever girl: "I cannot pretend . . . I never tell a lie . . . I have principles"— and all the time "I . . . I . . . I . . ."

N. is angry with his wife who is an actress, and without her knowledge gets abusive

paragraph, I am sure, is by no means aimed at Ibsen. Most probably the paragraph, as well as many others in the Notes, is something which C. either personally or indirectly heard someone say. You will see that Kuprin ["Reminiscences of Chekhov," by Gorky, Kuprin and Bunin, New York: Huebsch.] told C. the anecdote about the actor whose wife asked him to whistle a melody on the stage during a rehearsal. In C.'s Notes you have that anecdote, somewhat shortened and the names changed, without mentioning the source.

"The reader, on the whole, may puzzle his head over many paragraphs in the Notes, but he will hardly find explanations each time. What the reader has to remember is that the Notes are material used by C. in his creative activity and as such it throws a great deal of light on C.'s mentality and process of working."

criticisms published about her in the newspapers.

A nobleman boasts "This house of mine
was built in the time of Dmitry Donskoy."

"Your Worship, he called my dog a bad
name: 'son of a bitch.' "

The snow fell and did not lie on the
ground reddened with blood.

He left everything to charity, so that
nothing should go to his relations and children, whom he hated.

A very amorous man; he is no sooner
introduced to a girl than he becomes a he-
goat.

A nobleman Drekoliev.

I dread the idea that a chamberlain will
be present at the opening of my petition.

He was a rationalist, but he had to confess
that he liked the ringing of church bells.

The father a famous general, nice pictures, expensive furniture; he died; the daughters received a good education, but are slovenly, read little, ride, and are dull.

They are honest and truthful so long as it is unnecessary.

A rich merchant would like to have a shower bath in his W. C.

In the early morning they ate *okroshka*. [1]

"If you lose this talisman," said grandmother, "you will die." And suddenly I lost it, tortured myself, was afraid that I would die. And now, imagine, a miracle happened: I found it and continued to live.

Everybody goes to the theatre to see my play, to learn something instantly from it, to make some sort of profit, and I tell you: I have not the time to bother about that canaille.

[1] A cold dish composed of cider and hash.

The people hate and despise everything new and useful; when there was cholera, they hated and killed the doctors and they love vodka; by the people's love or hatred one can estimate the value of what they love or hate.

Looking out of the window at the corpse which is being borne to the cemetery: "You are dead, you are being carried to the cemetery, and I will go and have my breakfast."

A Tchech Vtitchka.

A man, forty years old, married a girl of twenty-two who read only the very latest writers, wore green ribbons, slept on yellow pillows, and believed in her taste and her opinions as if they were law; she is nice, not silly, and gentle, but he separates from her.

When one longs for a drink, it seems as though one could drink a whole ocean—that is faith; but when one begins to drink, one can only drink altogether two glasses—that is science.

For a farce: Fildekosov, Poprygunov.

In former times a nice man, with principles, who wanted to be respected, would try to become a general or priest, but now he goes in for being a writer, professor. . . .

There is nothing which history will not justify.

Zievoulia.

The crying of a nice child is ugly; so in bad verses you may recognize that the author is a nice man.

If you wish women to love you, be original; I know a man who used to wear felt boots summer and winter, and women fell in love with him.

I arrive at Yalta. Every room is engaged. I go to the "Italy"—not a room available. "What about my room number 35"—"It is engaged." A lady. They say: "Would you like to stay with this lady?

¹ A name or word invented by Chekhov meaning "One who yawns for a long time with pleasure."

The lady has no objection." I stay in her room. Conversation. Evening. The Tartar guide comes in. My ears are stopped, my eyes blindfolded; I sit and see nothing and hear nothing. . . .

A young lady complains: "My poor brother gets such a small salary—only seven thousand!"

She: "I see only one thing now: you have a large mouth! A large mouth! An enormous mouth!"

The horse is a useless and pernicious animal; a great deal of land has to be tilled for it, it accustoms man not to employ his own muscles, it is often an object of luxury; it makes man effeminate. For the future not a single horse.

N. a singer; speaks to nobody, his throat muffled up—he takes care of his voice, but no one has ever heard him sing.

About absolutely everything: "What's the good of that? It's useless!"

He wears felt boots summer and winter and gives this explanation: "It's better for the head, because the blood, owing to the heat, is drawn down into the feet, and the thoughts are clearer."

A woman is jocularly called Fiodor Ivanovitch.

A farce: N., in order to marry, greased the bald patch on his head with an ointment which he read of in an advertisement, and suddenly there began to grow on his head pig's bristles.

What does your husband do?—He takes castor oil.

A girl writes: "We shall live intolerably near you."

N. has been for long in love with Z. who married X.; two years after the marriage Z.

comes to N., cries, wishes to tell him something; N. expects to hear her complain against her husband; but it turns out that Z. has come to tell of her love for K.

N. a well known lawyer in Moscow; Z., who like N. was born in Taganrog, comes to Moscow and goes to see the celebrity; he is received warmly, but he remembers the school to which they both went, remembers how N. looked in his uniform, becomes agitated by envy, sees that N.'s flat is in bad taste, that N. himself talks a great deal; and he leaves disenchanted by envy and by the meanness which before he did not even suspect was in him.

The title of a play: The Bat.

Everything which the old cannot enjoy is forbidden or considered wrong.

When he was getting on in years, he married a very young girl, and so she faded and withered away with him.

All his life he wrote about capitalism and

millions, and he had never had any money.

A young lady fell in love with a handsome constable.

N. was a very good, fashionable tailor; but he was spoiled and ruined by trifles; at one time he made an overcoat without pockets, at another a collar which was much too high.

A farce: Agent of freight transport company and of fire insurance company.

Any one can write a play which might be produced.

A country house. Winter. N., ill, sits in his room. In the evening there suddenly arrives from the railway station a stranger Z., a young girl, who introduces herself and says that she has come to look after the invalid. He is perplexed, frightened, he refuses; then Z. says that at any rate she will stay the night. A day passes, two, and she goes on living there. She has an unbearable temper, she poisons one's existence.

A private room in a restaurant. A rich
man Z., tying his napkin round his neck,
touching the sturgeon with his fork: "At
least I'll have a snack before I die"—and he
has been saying this for a long time, daily.

By his remarks on Strindberg and literature generally L. L. Tolstoi reminds one very
much of Madam Loukhmav. [1]

Diedlov, when he speaks of the Deputy
Governor or the Governor, becomes a roman-
ticist, remembering "The Arrival of the
Deputy Governor" in the book *A Hundred
Russian Writers.*

A play: the Bean of Life.

A vet. belongs to the stallion class of
people.

Consultation.

The sun shines and in my soul is darkness.

[1] L. L. Tolstoi was Leo Nicolaievitch's son, Madame
Loukhmav a tenth rate woman writer.

In S. I made the acquaintance of the barrister Z.—a sort of Nika, The Fair. . . . He has several children; with all of them he is magisterial, gentle, kind, not a single rude word; I soon learn that he has another family. Then he invites me to his daughter's wedding; he prays, makes a genuflection, and says: "I still preserve religious feeling; I am a believer." And when in his presence people speak of education, of women, he has a naïve expression, exactly as if he did not understand. When he makes a speech in Court, his face looks as if he were praying.

"Mammy, don't show yourself to the guests, you are very fat."

Love? In love? Never! I am a Government clerk.

He knows little, even as a babe who has not yet come out of his mother's womb.

From childhood until extreme old age N. has had a passion for spying.

He uses clever words, that's all—philosophy . . . equator . . . (for a play).

The stars have gone out long ago, but they still shine for the crowd.

As soon as he became a scholar, he began to expect honors.

He was a prompter, but got disgusted and and gave it up; for about fifteen years he did not go to the theatre; then he went and saw a play, cried with emotion, felt sad, and, when his wife asked him on his return how he liked the theatre, he answered: "I do not like it."

The parlormaid Nadya fell in love with an exterminator of bugs and black beetles.

A Councillor of State; it came out after his death that, in order to earn a rouble, he was employed at the theatre to bark like a dog; he was poor.

You must have decent, well-dressed children, and your children too must have a nice house and children, and their children again children and nice houses; and what is it all for?—The devil knows.

Perkaturin.

Every day he forces himself to vomit—for the sake of his health, on the advice of a friend.

A Government official began to live an original life; a very tall chimney on his house, green trousers, blue waistcoat, a dyed dog, dinner at midnight; after a week he gave it up.

Success has already given that man a lick with its tongue.

In the bill presented by the hotel-keeper was among other things: "Bugs—fifteen kopecks." Explanation.

"N. has fallen into poverty."—"What? I can't hear."—"I say N. has fallen into poverty."—"What exactly do you say? I can't make out. What N.?"—"The N. who married Z."—"Well, what of it?" —"I say we ought to help him."—"Eh? What him? Why help? What do you mean?"—and so on.

How pleasant to sit at home, when the rain is drumming on the roof, and to feel that there are no heavy dull guests coming to one's house.

N. always even after five glasses of wine, takes valerian drops.

He lives with a parlormaid who respectfully calls him Your Honor.

I rented a country house for the summer; the owner, a very fat old lady, lived in the lodge, I in the great house; her husband was dead and so were all her children, she was left alone, very fat, the estate sold for debt, her furniture old and in good taste; all day long she reads letters which her husband and son had written to her. Yet she is an optimist. When some one fell ill in my house, she smiled and said again and again: "My dear, God will help."

N. and Z. are school friends, each seventeen or eighteen years old; and suddenly N. learns that Z. is with child by N.'s father.

The priezt came . . . zaint . . . praize
to thee, O Lord.

What empty words these discussions about
the rights of women! If a dog writes a
work of talent, they will even accept the dog.

Hæmorrhage: "It's an abscess that's just
burst inside you . . . it's all right, have some
more vodka."

The intelligentsia are good for nothing, because they drink a lot of tea, talk a lot in
stuffy rooms, with empty bottles.

When she was young, she ran away with a
doctor, a Jew, and had a daughter by him;
now she hates her past, hates the red-haired
daughter, and the father still loves her as
well as the daughter, and walks under her
window, chubby and handsome.

He picked his teeth and put the toothpick
back into the glass.

The husband and wife could not sleep;

they began to discuss how bad literature had become and how nice it would be to publish a magazine: the idea carried them away; they lay awake silent for awhile. "Shall we ask Boborykin to write?" he asked. "Certainly, do ask him." At five in the morning he starts for his work at the depot; she sees him off walking in the snow to the gate, shuts the gate after him. . . . "And shall we ask Potapenko?" he asks, already outside the gate.

When he learnt that his father had been raised to the nobility he began to sign himself Alexis.

Teacher: " 'The collision of a train with human victims' . . . that is wrong . . . it ought to be 'the collision of a train that resulted in human victims' . . . for the cause of the people on the line."

Title of play: Golden Rain.

There is not a single criterion which can serve as the measure of the non-existent, of the non-human.

[116]

A patriot: "And do you know that our Russian macaroni is better than the Italian? I'll prove it to you. Once at Nice they brought me sturgeon—do you know, I nearly cried." And the patriot did not see that he was only gastronomically patriotic.

A grumbler: "But is turkey food? Is caviare food?"

A very sensible, clever young woman; when she was bathing, he noticed that she had a narrow pelvis and pitifully thin hips—and he got to hate her.

A clock. Yegor the locksmith's clock at one time loses and at another gains exactly as if to spite him; deliberately it is now at twelve and then quite suddenly at eight. It does it out of animosity as though the devil were in it. The locksmith tries to find out the cause, and once he plunges it in holy water.

Formerly the heroes in novels and stories (e. g. Petchorin, Onyeguin) were twenty years old, but now one cannot have a hero

under thirty to thirty-five years.   The same
will soon happen with heroines.

N. is the son of a famous father; he is very
nice, but, whatever he does, every one says:
"That is very well, but it is nothing to the
father."   Once he gave a recitation at an
evening party; all the performers had a
success, but of him they said: "That is very
well, but still it is nothing to the father."
He went home and got into bed and, looking at his father's portrait, shook his fist at
him.

We fret ourselves to reform life, in order
that posterity may be happy, and posterity
will say as usual: "In the past it used to be
better, the present is worse than the past."

My motto: I don't want anything.

When a decent working-man takes himself and his work critically, people call him
grumbler, idler, bore; but when an idle
scoundrel shouts that it is necessary to work,
he is applauded.

promise. . . ." "A board which has the shape of a parallelepiped."

The hereditary honorable citizen Ozia-boushkin always tries to make out that his ancestors had the right to the title of Count.

"He is a perfect dab at it." "O, O, don't use that expression; my mother is very particular."

I have just married my third husband . . . the name of the first was Ivan Makarivitch . . . of the second Peter . . . Peter . . . I have forgotten."

The writer Gvozdikov thinks that he is very famous, that every one knows him. He arrives at S., meets an officer who shakes his hand for a long time, looking with rapture into his face. G. is glad, he too shakes hands warmly. . . . At last the officer: "And how is your orchestra? Aren't you the conductor?"

Morning; M.'s mustaches are in curl papers.

And it seemed to him that he was highly respected and valued everywhere, anywhere, even in railway buffets, and so he always ate with a smile on his face.

The birds sing, and already it begins to seem to him that they do not sing, but whine.

N., father of a family, listens to his son reading aloud J. J. Rousseau to the family, and thinks: "Well, at any rate, J. J. Rousseau had no gold medal on his breast, but I have one."

N. has a spree with his step-son, an undergraduate, and they go to a brothel. In the morning the undergraduate is going away, his leave is up; N. sees him off. The undergraduate reads him a sermon on their bad behavior; they quarrel. N: "As your father, I curse you."—"And I curse you."

A doctor is called in, but a nurse sent for.

N. N. V. never agrees with anyone: "Yes, the ceiling is white, that can be admitted; but white, as far as is known, consists of the seven colors of the spectrum, and it is quite possible that in this case one of the colors is darker or brighter than is necessary for the production of pure white; I had rather think a bit before saying that the ceiling is white."

He holds himself exactly as though he were an icon.

"Are you in love?"—"There's a little bit of that in it."

Whatever happens, he says: "It is the priests."

Firzikov.

N. dreams that he is returning from abroad, and that at Verzhbolovo, in spite of his protests, they make him pay duty on his wife.

When that radical, having dined with his coat off, walked into his bedroom and I saw

[123]

the braces on his back, it became clear to me that that radical is a bourgeois, a hopeless bourgeois.

Some one saw Z., an unbeliever and blasphemer, secretly praying in front of the icon in the cathedral, and they all teased him.

They called the manager "four-funneled cruiser," because he had already gone "through the chimney" (bankrupt) four times.

He is not stupid, he was at the university, has studied long and assiduously, but in writing he makes gross mistakes.

Countess Nadin's daughter gradually turns into a housekeeper; she is very timid, and can only say "No-o," "Yes-s," and her hands always tremble. Somehow or other a Zemstvo official wished to marry her; he is a widower and she marries him, with him too it was "Yes-s," "No-o"; she was very much afraid of her husband and did not love him; one day he happened to give a loud cough, it gave her a fright, and she died.

Caressing her lover: "My vulture."

For a play: If only you would say something funny. But for twenty years we have lived together and you have always talked of serious things; I hate serious things.

A cook, with a cigarette in her mouth, lies: "I studied at a high school . . . I know what for the earth is round."

"Society for finding and raising anchors of steamers and barges," and the Society's agent at all functions without fail makes a speech, à la N., and without fail promises.

Super-mysticism.

When I become rich, I shall have a harem in which I shall keep fat naked women, with their buttocks painted green.

A shy young man came on a visit for the night: suddenly a deaf old woman came into his room, carrying a cupping-glass, and bled

him; he thought that this must be the usual
thing and so did not protest; in the morning
it turned out that the old woman had made a
mistake.

Surname: Verstax.

The more stupid the peasant, the better
does the horse understand him.

THEMES, THOUGHTS, NOTES, AND
FRAGMENTS.

. . . How stupid and for the most part how false, since if one man seeks to devour another or tell him something unpleasant it has nothing to do with Granovsky.[1]

I left Gregory Ivanovitch's feeling crushed and mortally offended. I was irritated by smooth words and by those who speak them, and on reaching home I meditated thus: some rail at the world, others at the crowd, that is to say praise the past and blame the present; they cry out that there are no ideals and so on, but all this has already been said twenty or thirty years ago; these are worn-out forms which have already served their time, and whoever repeats them now, he too is no longer young and is himself worn out. With last year's foliage there decay too those who live in it. I thought, we uncultured, worn-out people, banal in speech, stereotyped in intentions, have grown quite mouldy, and, while we intellectuals are rummaging among old rags

[1] A well-known Radical professor, a Westerner.

[129]

and, according to the old Russian custom, biting one another, there is boiling up around us a life which we neither know nor notice. Great events will take us unawares, like sleeping fairies, and you will see that Sidorov, the merchant, and the teacher of the school at Yeletz, who see and know more than we do, will push us far into the background, because they will accomplish more than all of us put together. And I thought that were we now to obtain political liberty, of which we talk so much, while engaged in biting one another, we should not know what to do with it, we should waste it in accusing one another in the newspapers of being spies and money-grubbers, we should frighten society with the assurance that we have neither men, nor science, nor literature, nothing! Nothing! And to scare society as we are doing now, and as we shall continue to do, means to deprive it of courage; it means simply to declare that we have no social or political sense in us. And I also thought that, before the dawn of a new life has broken, we shall turn into sinister old men and women and we shall be the first who, in our hatred of that dawn, will calumniate it.

Mother never stops talking about poverty. It is very strange. In the first place, it is strange that we are poor, beg like beggars, and at the same time eat superbly, live in a large house; in the summer we go to our own country house, and generally speaking we do not look like beggars. Evidently this is not poverty, but something else, and rather worse. Secondly, it is strange that for the last ten years mother has been spending all her energy solely on getting money to pay interest. It seems to me that were mother to spend that terrible energy on something else, we could have twenty such houses. Thirdly, it seems to me strange that the hardest work in the family is done by mother, not by me. To me that is the strangest thing of all, most terrible. She has, as she has just said, a thought on her brain, she begs, she humiliates herself; our debts grow daily and up till now I have not done a single thing to help her. What can I do? I think and think and cannot make it out. I only see clearly that we are rushing down an inclined plane, but to what, the devil knows. They say that poverty threatens us and that in poverty there is disgrace, but that too I cannot understand, since I was never poor.

The spiritual life of these women is as gray and dull as their faces and dresses; they speak of science, literature, tendencies, and the like, only because they are the wives and sisters of scholars and literary men; were they the wives and sisters of inspectors or of dentists, they would speak with the same zeal of fires or teeth. To allow them to speak of science, which is foreign to them, and to listen to them, is to flatter their ignorance.

Essentially all this is crude and meaningless, and romantic love appears as meaningless as an avalanche which involuntarily rolls down a mountain and overwhelms people. But when one listens to music, all this is: that some people lie in their graves and sleep, and that one woman is alive—grayhaired, she is sitting in a box in the theatre, quiet and majestic, and the avalanche seems no longer meaningless, since in nature everything has a meaning. And everything is forgiven, and it would be strange not to forgive.

Olga Ivanovna regarded old chairs, stools, sofas, with the same respectful tenderness as she regarded old dogs and horses, and her room, therefore, was something like an almshouse for furniture. Round the mirror, on all tables and shelves, stood photographs of uninteresting, half-forgotten people; on the walls hung pictures at which nobody ever looked; and it was always dark in the room, because there burnt there only one lamp with a blue shade.

If you cry "Forward," you must without fail explain in which direction one must go. Do you not see that, if without explaining the direction, you fire off this word simultaneously at a monk and at a revolutionary, they will proceed in precisely opposite directions?

It is said in Holy Writ: "Fathers, do not irritate your children," even the wicked and good-for-nothing children; but the fathers irritate me, irritate me terribly. My contemporaries chime in with them and the youngsters follow, and every minute they strike me in the face with their smooth words.

That the aunt suffered and did not show it gave him the impression of a trick.

O. I. was in constant motion; such women, like bees, carry about a fertilizing pollen. . . .

Don't marry a rich woman—she will drive you out of the house; don't marry a poor woman—you won't sleep; but marry the freest freedom, the lot and life of a Cossack. (Ukrainian saying.)

Aliosha: "I often hear people say: 'Before marriage there is romance, and then—goodbye, illusion!' How heartless and coarse it is."

So long as a man likes the splashing of a fish, he is a poet; but when he knows that the splashing is nothing but the chase of the weak by the strong, he is a thinker; but when he does not understand what sense there is in the chase, or what use in the equilibrium which results from destruction, he is becoming silly and dull, as he was when a child. And the more he knows and thinks, the sillier he becomes.

The death of a child. I have no sooner sat down in peace than—bang—fate lets fly at me.

The she-wolf, nervous and anxious, fond of her young, dragged away a foal into her winter-shelter, thinking him a lamb. She knew that there was a ewe there and that the ewe had young. While she was dragging the foal away, suddenly some one whistled; she was alarmed and dropped him, but he followed her. They arrived at the shelter. He began to suck like the young wolves. Throughout the winter he changed but little; he only grew thin and his legs longer, and the spot on his forehead turned into a triangle. The she-wolf was in delicate health.[1]

They invited celebrities to these evening parties, and it was dull because there are few

[1] A sketch of part of the story "Whitehead."

people of talent in Moscow, and the same singers and reciters performed at all evening parties.

She has not before felt herself so free and easy with a man.

You wait until you grow up and I'll teach you declamation.

It seemed to her that at the show many of the pictures were alike.

There filed up before you a whole line of laundry-maids.

Kostya insisted that the women had robbed themselves.

L. put himself in the place of the juryman and interpreted it thus: if it was a case of house-breaking, then there was no theft, because the laundresses themselves sold the linen and spent the money on drink; but if it was a case of theft, then there could have been no house-breaking.

[136]

Fiodor was flattered that his brother had found him at the same table with a famous actor.

When Y. spoke or ate, his beard moved as if he had no teeth in his mouth.

Ivashin loved Nadya Vishnyevsky and was afraid of his love. When the butler told him that the old lady had just gone out, but the young lady was at home, he fumbled in his fur coat and dress-coat pocket, found his card, and said: "Right."

But it was not all right. Driving from his house in the morning, to pay a visit, he thought that he was compelled to it by conventions of society, which weighed heavily upon him. But now it was clear to him that he went to pay calls only because somewhere far away in the depths of his soul, as under a veil, there lay hidden a hope that he would see Nadya. . . . And he suddenly felt pitiful, sad, and a little frightened. . . .

In his soul, it seemed to him, it was snowing, and everything faded away. He was afraid to love Nadya, because he was too old

[137]

for her, thought his appearance unattractive, and did not believe that young girls like Nadya could love men for their minds and spiritual qualities. Still there would at times rise in him something like a hope. But now, from the moment when the officer's spurs jingled and then died away, there also died away his timid love. . . . All was at an end, hope was impossible. . . . "Yes, now all is finished," he thought, "I am glad, very glad."

He imagined his wife to be not Nadya, but always, for some reason, a stout woman with a large bosom, covered with Venetian lace.

The clerks in the office of the Governor of the island have a drunken headache. They long for a drink. They have no money. What is to be done? One of them, a convict who is serving his time here for forgery, devises a plan. He goes to the church, where a former officer, now exiled for giving his superior a box on the ears, sings in the choir, and says to him panting: "Here!

There's a pardon come for you! They have got a telegram in the office."

The late officer turns pale, trembles, and can hardly walk for excitement.

"But for such news you ought to give something for a drink," says the clerk.

"Take all I have! All!"

And he hands him some five roubles. . . . He arrives at the office. The officer is afraid that he may die from joy and presses his hand to his heart.

"Where is the telegram?"

"The bookkeeper has put it away." (He goes to the bookkeeper.) General laughter and an invitation to drink with them.

"How terrible!"

After that the officer was ill for a week.[1]

Fedya, the steward's brother-in-law, told Ivanov that wild-duck were feeding on the other side of the wood. He loaded his gun with slugs. Suddenly a wolf appeared. He fired and smashed both the wolf's hips. The wolf was mad with pain and did not see

[1] An episode which Chekhov heard during his journey in the island, Saghalien.

him. "What can I do for you, dear?" He
thought and thought, and then went home
and called Peter. . . . Peter took a stick,
and with an awful grimace, began to beat
the wolf. . . . He beat and beat and beat
until it died. . . . He broke into a sweat
and went away, without saying a single
word.

Vera: "I do not respect you, because you
married so strangely, because nothing came
of you. . . . That is why I have secrets
from you."

It is unfortunate that we try to solve the
simplest questions cleverly, and therefore
make them unusually complicated. We
should seek a simple solution.

There is no Monday which will not give
its place to Tuesday.

I am happy and satisfied, sister, but if I
were born a second time and were asked:
"Do you want to marry?" I should answer:
"No." "Do you want to have money?"
"No. . . ."

Lenstchka liked dukes and counts in novels, not ordinary persons. She loved the chapters in which there is love, pure and ideal not sensual. Descriptions of nature she did not like. She preferred conversations to descriptions. While reading the beginning she would glance impatiently at the end. She did not remember the names of authors. She wrote with a pencil in the margins: "Wonderful!" "Beautiful!" or "Serve him right!"

Lenstehka sang without opening her mouth.

Post coitum: We Balderiovs always excelled in vigor and health.

He drove in a cab, and, as he watched his son walking away, thought: "Perhaps, he belongs to the race of men who will no longer trundle in scurvy cabs, as I do, but will fly through the skies in balloons."

She is so beautiful that it is even frightening; dark eye-brows.

The son says nothing, but the wife feels him to be an enemy; she feels that he has overheard everything. . . .

What a lot of idiots there are among ladies. People get so used to it that they do not notice it.

They often go to the theatre and read serious magazines—and yet are spiteful and immoral.

Nat: "I never have fits of hysterics. I am not a pampered darling." [1]

Nat: (continually to her sisters): "O, how ugly you have grown. O, how old you do look!"

To live one must have something to hang on to. . . . In the provinces only the body works, not the spirit.

You won't become a saint through other people's sins.

[1] This and the following few passages are from the rough draft of Chekhov's play *Three Sisters*.

Koulyguin: "I am a jolly fellow, I infect every one with my mood."

Koul. Gives lessons at rich houses.

Koul. In Act IV without mustaches.

The wife implores the husband: "Don't get fat."

O if there were a life in which every one grew younger and more beautiful.

Irene: "It is hard to live without a father, without a mother."—"And without a husband."—"Yes, without a husband. Whom could one confide in? To whom could one complain? With whom could one share ones's joy? One must love some one strongly."

Koulyguin (to his wife): "I am so happy to be married to you, that I consider it ungentlemanly and improper to speak of or even mention a dowry. Hush, don't say anything. . . ."

The doctor enjoys being at the duel.

It is difficult to live without orderlies. You cannot make the servants answer your bell.

The 2nd, 3rd, and 6th companies left at 4, and we leave at 12 sharp. [1]

In the daytime conversations about the loose manners of the girls in secondary schools, in the evening a lecture on degeneration and the decline of everything, and at night, after all this, one longs to shoot oneself.

In the life of our towns there is no pessimism, no Marxism, and no movements, but there is stagnation, stupidity, mediocrity.

He had a thirst for life, but it seemed to him to mean that he wanted a drink—and he drank wine.

F. in the town-hall: Serguey Nik. in a

[1] Here the fragments from the rough draft of *Three Sisters* end.

plaintive voice: "Gentlemen, where can we get the means? Our town is poor."

To be idle involuntarily means to listen to what is being said, to see what is being done; but he who works and is occupied hears little and sees little.

In the skating rink he raced after L.; he wanted to overtake her and it seemed as if it were life which he wanted to overtake, that life which one cannot bring back or overtake or catch, just as one cannot catch one's shadow.

Only one thought reconciled him to the doctor: just as he had suffered from the doctor's ignorance, so perhaps some one was suffering from his mistakes.

But isn't it strange? In the whole town there is not a single musician, not a single orator, not a prominent man.

Honorable Justice of the Peace, Honorable Member of the Children's Shelter—all honorable.

[145]

L. studied and studied—but people who had finished developing could not understand her, nor could the young. *Ut consecutivum.*

He is dark, with little side-whiskers, dressed like a dandy, dark eyes, a warm brunet. He exterminates bugs, talks about earthquakes and China. His fiancée has a dowry of 8,000 roubles; she is very handsome, as her aunt says. He is an agent for a fire-insurance company, etc. "You're awfully pretty, my darling, awfully. And 8,000 into the bargain! You are a beauty; when I looked at you to-day, a shiver ran down my back."

He: Earthquakes are caused by the evaporation of water.

Names: Goose, Pan, Oyster.
"Were I abroad, they would give me a medal for such a surname."

I can't be said to be handsome, but I am rather pretty.

[146]